I SAW THE BEST MEMES OF MY GENERATION

T0359278

I SAW THE BEST MEMES OF MY GENERATION

DOMINIC SYMES

RECENT
WORK
PRESS

I Saw the Best Memes of My Generation
Recent Work Press
Canberra, Australia

Copyright © Dominic Symes, 2022

ISBN: 9780645356366 (paperback)

 A catalogue record for this
book is available from the
National Library of Australia

All rights reserved. This book is copyright. Except for private study,
research, criticism or reviews as permitted under the Copyright Act,
no part of this book may be reproduced, stored in a retrieval system,
or transmitted in any form by any means without prior written
permission. Enquiries should be addressed to the publisher.

Cover image: 'The empty bag' (2021) by Jean Bergeron as part of the
Vie pub_like project, a daily experimental work in progress project.
Used with permission of the artist. @vie_pub_like
Cover design: Recent Work Press
Set by Recent Work Press

recentworkpress.com

Contents

Algorithm

stood before an automated door
that refused to acknowledge my existence
I thought
but I'm *here*

& yes
I do remember when time online was
less anxious—not a threat
to national security
      democracy

of course
an election is not a cake walk
though strolling & scrolling both
have an idleness inbuilt

the hand towel dispenser
unfurls itself
then stops
as if to say
that's enough now

even flags
patrolling the breeze
maintain this ironic curl of their lips
as they salute

in the book I'm reading
Shelley has written a letter
accounting for the FOUR DAYS
it will take to reach Mary

to say that he will see her again
in TEN

instead I give you everything
all the time
my metadata

& yes I recall when
I wasn't so scared to share
whatever   was on my mind
with whoever   happened
to be online   at the time

ask me anything
I had written

anything?

now I watch the candle
folding in upon itself
anxiously encoding its light
upon the ceiling of my bedroom

while I'm up all night
deleting statuses from when I was 19
in case I ever want to get a job

Sonnet (Now Now)

purple sky I see you
the stove glows itself down
chuckling myself back up the stairs
dynamic as they are   these waves
which keep me from reaching you
it is the day before my birthday
& the maths   have found their way inside
again   I am growing older   certainly
but instead of a curtain's opacity
all of a sudden I want to be urgent
& un-ironic   *this dark heart is vainly craving*
so I'll leave you these venetians
   29th of June
   29 years since the velvet revolution

I don't normally leave reviews for my Airbnb hosts, but since they insisted

the wi-fi exceeded expectations

& now I'm stuck for anything else to say. I'm trying to write this review before checking out, sitting on a bamboo mat on a floor in Yogyakarta. I could have spent all night kissing the smog from your mouth & spitting it back into the brown river, but instead we lulled the rats to sleep with our whispered suspicions, utterly in awe of their roof-shattering romantic aggressions, infinitely better suited to the conditions. Maybe it was just karma biting us back for lying to our host when we told her it was our honeymoon, but we didn't want to be disturbed & were kinda hoping that we'd get a discount. Plus, we knew we'd be leaving soon & couldn't have anticipated she'd ask to see our wedding photos. So, we stayed up, unsleeping, to watch each other sweat above the sheets in this tiny bedroom without a mosquito net or an air conditioner, but I guess it's best not to mention that.

the teak furniture was beautiful

    & it was

The Coffee Coffee Drinks

'Fortis ut mors dilectio"
—the Song of Solomon, as inscribed on a necklace my Apinko
  gave my Maminka on their engagement.

love is as strong as death
                                        —this coffee is at least

                 though when the flickering bickering of a lifetime
                       is gathered up
                                    it is unable to fill even a single cup

        kept   in the small heart-shaped chamber
                             of the house you carry with you
                       everywhere

             we're as close as jeans & skin
                                        —like lint

        collecting one another from the airport
                       a week apart   we sit together now
                          in the shuddering depths of night

           watching the staff head home exhausted
    from straddling time zones
                                   from being so polite

        joint like a bank account   our money
           is the same money
                             even when the interest
           rate is variable:
                       where do I put it all?

5

where does it fit
               this misplaced romantic intensity?

the libraries are full
                                        & galleries
preach a learned disinterestedness

this will be an everlasting love

sings the cartoon baby bird
                              discovering its voice

loving you makes me not believe in miracles

but in life   & death   turning over

like the pedals on your pushbike   loudly

declaring their decay   & rust

everything tastes sweeter in the dark
                                        that trust
is earned
              —you learn
                   not   to ignore the symptoms

but to relish instead your diagnosis:

                          to love the love you know

Greta Thunberg Ode

children the size of adults
   pester me with questions like

     how big is *your* carbon footprint?

I mean   yes
                I'm a minor poet

     not a major corporation

   but I'd still prefer being
        taken to task by someone
   with a stake in the future

 over being taken to court

  watching the lawyers
stride in
 & out of the stone building

         from the shade of this
        frankly arrogant
        very upright tree

    there is a whiff of the
      entitlement that comes off
   a certain kind of person
   who when asked

   still or sparkling

answers

      sparkling

              or
           something equally
        as bougie

  is firing off tweets
as bad as burning down
 forests?

        I mean
           I get it
      some kids don't want to have to
       think about the Anthropocene

they want Gazelles
            Jordans

  they want Supreme

I
  on the other hand

grew up
      climbing trees

  barefoot & in rags
swinging off
  the Moreton Bay figs
outside the zoo

       a real Mowgli figure
     of inner suburban Adelaide

imagining the tree
  was my mother

        or at least the female
           tree-character from
        Pocahontas

(…it's Grandmother Willow, but I had to IMDb it)

when
      you stop to think
        for a minute
            that's a strange film

I mean
      from a postcolonial perspective

    there's settlement
  & white entitlement
      not to mention
        extensive
            land clearing

  plus   it stars

    Mel Gibson
          before he got cancelled

        for saying those
      awful things about
        Jewish people

  —my point being

can the market
really be relied upon
to even all of this out?

to absorb our   stupidity

the way   trees
absorb our carbon
from the
atmosphere?

can a pouch of tobacco
costing $36
really stop someone
from smoking?

can e-cigarettes?

can this 36 degree day
lived here
that could be anywhere
somewhere in
the golden age of capitalism?

golden
in the way that
a plant turns golden when the sun
had voided it
of its moisture?

golden
in the way that as a society
we tend
to convince ourselves

things are beautiful
        even as they're
    dying
            right in front
            of our eyes?

                        I've been
                            having better conversations
                        since accepting this
                            perennial state of
                        emergency

        reading about the school
        protests & watching Greta
    Thunberg videos on YouTube

    accepting the
solution will not be simple
    or easy

                    as
                    unpalatable as it
                    tastes

                this soy latte
            is not the solution

with the newspaper
    in front of me
                    which I'm sure
                almost no one my age
                    or younger
                is reading

the editorial suggests

maybe plant a tree?

or *get a SodaStream?*

failing that
their logic would
advocate

*just go back to work
as normal?*

& if you don't have a job

buy one?

Queering the Cannon

I love the phrase *queering the canon*
because it always makes me think of Cher

even though I know it's not *that* kind of cannon
every time someone says it all I can see
is her on that battleship in a leotard
queering the *fuck* out of the cannon

this may mean nothing here
but everyone should read the poet Thom Gunn
for the Apollonian form
& for the Dionysian content
    psychotropics never hit harder than
when experienced through iambs

how Larkin said the 'h' in Thom was only there to confuse
but then Larkin *would* say that

fair play—I like his jazz criticism
yet I can't get past the thought that
he probably masturbated a lot
or at least was a slave to some
delightful kink

it's ok if right now you're imagining Larkin
astride a cannon in a leotard

the canon often inserts itself unwantedly into conversation

I talk to students too young to understand my niche references
& too old & too smart to listen to anything I have to say

like this ad from my childhood
we got on like a house on fire
until the house literally caught on fire

The Rolling Stones have always been old to me
though I love the rumour that Jagger & Bowie were an item

I've been instructed by The Guardian—

                                    which I pay for now
after being guilted by that widget which kept telling me how
many free articles I'd read   & which I'll admit
feels kind of like paying a bully at school to stop you from
getting beat up   (I believe that is called a 'racket')

                    —to feminise the canon

it's like the Hells Angels telling the Stones
they couldn't go on stage in San Francisco
because they'd just stabbed someone in the front row

trust? the ad goes
                    who can you?

I worked in an English department with only female lecturers
& tutors while all the profs were male & getting paid more
unsurprisingly when I taught Romantic literature it seemed
all the texts were by male authors

except for those by Anna Leticia Barbauld   Mary Shelley
Mary Shelley's mum   Mary Godwin
all three Brontë sisters (the 'ë' only there to confuse)
Austen obviously

actually   charge up queens

I like the way being surrounded by good art
is like being surrounded by a thousand camp sailors
on a battleship

   queer & comforting

July Poem

how strange & Viennese you are today Adelaide
like the skating rink installed in front of the Rathausplatz

here I am finding it hard to stay upright too
a tourist in my own city
every step I take is cautious
        though ambulant
    still moving

I wonder if it's a frozen river
that I'm skating on
  —the Blue Danube?
or a smaller tributary
    building to crescendo?

of course after the rain last week the Torrens
is covered over with a layer of earth
silt
  like sheets of brown ice shifting
glacially
    patiently

   it's the black swans
traversing pontoons of leaf litter with
circumspect
     spindly legs

it's an abandoned bike I see
  the same single speed
that I have walked past for weeks now

    chained to the thin trunk
of a plane tree by the smokers' tables

it's these same barren trees that
deciduous
                  arthritic
creak & bend in the wind
but won't uproot

walking between the Exeter & the old hospital
past the Elephant & the Palace Nova
it's the sun
        low in the sky that warms my back

& it's the light
               that like a tourist bends down
& tries to pick out one of the dollar coins
        embedded in the footpath

that makes me think this is all
                  positively Hapsburgian

Hallelujah Junction

they are stacking up the chairs at the Exeter
as we walk out of the cinema
I'm a sucker for endings

those parting tears   from the perspective
    of an open fireplace
remember us to the balmy night

nothing is supposed to last forever
& shouldn't this be liberating?

my fingers play this conversation
as Schubert   as a young Mozart
as a fleeting thought
            as exit music for a film

a song for the flies that rest on your unbuttoned shirt
& the words that transform your tongue into a foreign body
a song the sound of your piss in the bathroom

with the curtains drawn
slides pass across the wall
these brief moments of stillness
    these antiquated forms
        we learn by touch alone

in your bed we have another conversation
remaining staunchly theoretical
right up until the moment I fall asleep
    on your chest

I hear the call for last drinks
ringing through the alley
though I'm hardly here

        I'm with you
in that remembered summer

my heart is like the skin of a peach
in the blazing afternoon
go ahead
& fuck me up

Fucking Adelaide

as white as the paper I've been handed
no matter how I drag myself through the dirt
your white noise is only ever shifting register

wet splendour of North Terrace at 5pm
glass of water? I ask shielding my eyes
while a roomful of aspiring artists smoulder
in front of your stretch marks

your bare shoulders square up
like a painting while our attention
gets drawn away from the edges
so expertly

I wait for the tattoo of first knowing you
to become as smooth as skin again

the cranes play off the reflected skyline
sounding out your sprawl of endless deferral
on the ground as the protest disperses
some of us go back to study & some of us go drinking

like Pound says poetry requires the energy of a lifetime
—getting drunk is more than one day's work

a polaroid of us & I'm drawing ears on you
so big you'll hear me being born! come spill over
these rusted gutters with me!

piles of days too hot to move cool & coagulate like cars
becoming traffic as the rain turns our watches soft

peak hour evokes the short twentieth century:
euro-centric & my friends still smoke
I'd rather forget all about it   except for the sun
on your Germanic shoulders   this girl   who's just like you
but with a bigger mouth   early Shostakovich   & this jumper
that I've had since you gave it to me on the bus to Skyshow

my arms prickle when I'm indoors
though I enjoy the rain when it's on my lips
my eyelashes
        my epaulets

earrings the size of trees hang on the street emitting
faulty golden light

I'm learning to make you laugh all over again
now that we aren't sleeping together anymore
cruising the banks of the river alone

when I speak to you about the stars
you excuse yourself for sneezing
wipers drag across the windscreen
they do nothing to remove the hot breath
of our whispers

walking home
you pick me
a sprig of jasmine
still heavy with rain

                I smell it now

Scatole Personali

(After Robert Rauschenberg)

Rome opens its doors
but is never around
when I choose to stay in

     so in a way
     we miss each other
     but still I get to enjoy
     sifting through cupboards
     & using the free wi-fi

I figure
it's a shame I can't draw

          this would be the perfect park
          to sketch portraits in

laying on my elbow
a closed bracket

     the curved terrace
     of houses in this quarter

the way grass
cheap wine
& the afternoon
do their best to stop you
in your tracks

     in their wake

walking through the cemetery
looking for Keats

finding out the
significant difference
between
a sculpture & a headstone

between
a mausoleum & a museum

timing
matters less
drinking it in
as we are
here

you are here
with me

on a much-photographed balcony
of yesterday

& today
the flowers in this terracotta
pot have not changed much

a view of the colosseum
holding still

our most recent
disagreement is over
definition
& destination

I like seeing likeness
in the throes of morning
waking up when I am you
until I come back
from the bathroom
a little more me

warm sun
on this balcony
recalls a distant ache

blinding
that deep ember
it comes to unfuck the morning

as I'm taut
& shimmering

shaking like wires above a tram
transformed by
misplaced electricity

in the whirr of a laptop opening
a kettle peaking

the coffee comes
only a little
more bitter
than the day before

cafés
marking each hour of the morning

the piazza
sets one against the other
as if fixed hinges on a sundial
time stands still

watching locals
enjoy their toast
smothered in thick jam

taking pictures of one another
waiting on the gutter

ads on the park bench
& discount stores
diabetic with colour
tiny bottles of spirits & souvenirs
I don't need

walking out of the restaurant
into the eternal city

lights in this hallway
persistent
on the marble floor

our footsteps
as the rain slides off us
half drunk

carafes left on the table
returning from dinner

each night moves me
closer to the next

dissolving
like heat does from the shadow
cast by the church's reach

walking
back to the pensione
around the colosseum
as the sun is coming up
the streets are still beautiful
sleeping

      & perhaps that's the closest
      I'll get to feel you breathing

roller doors return
to queues reforming
my love of language
formed by a lack
of understanding

      breathing
      is not one's signature

this is the long way of getting to the gallery
I take it

      like those sculptures in the foyer
      that don't really announce themselves
      as sculptures
      by their conversation

I'm taking pictures
of the floor

sparrows
gossiping on the window

the chlorine green fountain
that sits switched off
in September

where pizzas come an hour late
& a metre long

the alley
where we argue even longer
too early for Aperol

not a colour as much as
it is a surface tension

painting over is painting
just the same

the impression
of rain

how it reacts with marble
turning it dark
pressing itself deep
into the crevices

self-portrait in Monte
in the light above this mirror
that must be new

& I have never known myself so well

this greying man
asks me to open the window
on the moving train

my poor Italian is mistaken for
awe-struck humility
rushing in

there is no music in this bedsit
but the twinkle of my keys
on the bedside table

a block away
from the main square

a set of stairs
has outlived whatever
it once led to

& is in that way
artistic

birds at the café
sparrows
dipping their beaks into
cups so small
the novelty disappears

one sips a short black
opaque
on the counter

leaving very quickly

tumbling through the tight streets
our argument

    follows all this way

vague sound of a mambo
playing through a portable radio
sauntering drunkenly through

      archways
      like aqueducts
      beneath people's houses

& isn't it great
the echoing
smell of it all
old stone

      holy water
      from a crumbling font

the atmosphere
of autobiography lingers

      loose knots
      tied up
      lay useless on the pier

belief as only an ochre sky
can give

        as those last boats
        return

tracing the gesture of the wind
in the act of tracing

      sustaining an ellipsis
      of white birds trailing off

a message carried home

        to every bar
        we are welcomed in
        with salt
        to stop us leaving

licking your lips
in your sleep

      children on the street
      walk up to you
      & smother you with orange
      prosecco kisses

like you're a lowkey movie star
or a tourist in the 60s

      heat
      trapped in the corso

rising up through our seats
translates
as tingling in our cheeks

      riding home
      from the beach
      white line of salt
      drying into our clothes

the water keeps us
wide eyed for sleep

    the day does nothing
    but strip itself away
    revolving to escape the sun
    but only briefly

sky stretched as tight as skin
the clouds
wish to be considered
overlook what the ocean

    the sound never travels
    as far away
    as I am from

an invitation
extending almost
to the horizon's
burnt edge

    the bay
    deep green lines etched
    into the hillside
    wind their way skyward

an irregular flicker of lights
trailing up the side
reappearing from hairpins

    the glow & hum of Napoli
    behind the hills

waiting for us

ocean turns the colour of possibility
a hot purple-pink
holding desperately on to the last light
of the afternoon

       a fish shop's blue neon
       the flashing red & green

traffic lights
on the street below

       soon there is nothing
       but a palette of shades
       mixed together
       in the darkened room

watching you sleep is like watching
wine in a glass

       primed for anything
       this too has colour

Machu Picchu

on the edge of a dream where everything unfinished
remains for you to return to   like a message you *saw*
but chose to leave unseen—unread, I mean

you are instead the one left blue
at a skating rink & shivering awkwardly
on a first date, your first ever

what I would say to you
    —what I would say now to anyone under 25—is
no one in human history has ever stayed out past 5am
chatting, sitting next to someone they find attractive
& not woken up the next morning more in love

it would be like walking up to Machu Picchu
& failing to take a picture

moving   so lightly   through space

like Sarah who actually knew how to skate
carving beautiful lines
impossible for you to follow
though you tried

you look at your watch & you aren't even tired

you think
I could have gone home
so   many   times   already
but you didn't & now the sun
coming up
over the city

makes it look
abandoned for centuries

emptied out
except for her

that's what it felt like the first time

For Frank & Lillian on the Occasion of Their Wedding

as the shot clock drops to single digits

it's strange   you think
  how in the countdown to launch
    the numbers never quite
empty out to zero

                    —they just say *lift off*

whereas on a commercial plane
you can choose   *welcome home*
    or   *enjoy your stay*

              usually only one applies

but in this strange new city you get both
    upon arrival

that release

                              like a sparkler that spits
                          fizzes & glows forever
                      even in the daylight

or a packet of timtams
that comes with its own genie
    to grant you more timtams

even when you have a tummy ache
  or early onset diabetes

Hydra

friends as old as philosophy
red wine & an azure horizon
set against the hot white cliffs
a kiss on either cheek comes
a side plate of fried cheese
& slices of very crusty bread
while I chronicle the exact quality
of the sunlight which
illuminates our faces
our own deeply held views
reflected back at us
in the exposed midriff
of another cloudless day
this one olive tree is everything
expressible in language
living together in this dappled light
sipping cheap local beer served to us
in small glasses that soon populate the table
open collars & a peaceful breeze
from the parched hilltops
while a single lightbulb above us
is the alpha & omega of night
a counterpoint to every metaphor
which passes for logic
whole days go by
where we only talk about one another
& what's for dinner tonight
—what record will we get out
of our chairs drunk
& dance to

Masculinities

he hugs his opponent
grasping really at himself
the sweat & blood commingles
to mask the tears that swell like bitten lips
his head at rest on his shoulder
out to kill the mess of pronouns
which in the hard relief of this moment
are indiscernible
clothes shed on a bedroom floor
like a waterfall in slow motion
acknowledging the body's limit
a cascade of limbs burning
seeing the dust lift itself
off the canvas that pit of fire
spitting embers
while he should be keeping well away
instead he steps
behind the sheet of water
& into the cavern of noise
reverberating through the still air
as the referee steps in
pulling them apart

Tiergarten / Doc Martens

under Aquarius stars spit out light
like broken teeth
you sleep beside me
punch drunk
& sickly sweet
like peach schnapps
how we stumbled home together
licking our lips
in our double laced docs
kicking snow to the curb
as if offcuts   shavings
dust from the stars
       blacking out
       & falling at our feet

Speeding Up & Slowing Down

there's immense pleasure to be had
speeding up
                    & slowing down

in   waking yourself up
before you're really awake

in pulling the train's emergency brake

launching yourself
    into a cold shower
                 or an icy lake

picking up a log off of the fire
          for a laugh with your mates

I think about ripping up the handbrake
on my best friend's mum's Daihatsu
on the way to school

snaking our way through the teachers' car park

arrested in motion together

not yet before the principal

it's seeing a magician on the television at your uncle's place & yanking
the tablecloth out from underneath the set table just the same in your
imagination & shaking you out
of your ruminations

the pilot jams on the thrusters
as the plane nears the end of its descent
to even up the wheels

like being overfed but undernourished
coming down too fast
from a sugar high

until you're watching daylight pass
through the soft fabric of the curtains
making beautiful jellyfish
silhouettes over the parquetry
on the edge of falling asleep
having spent the afternoon
sweeping up the thousand shards
of your too fragile
bohemian crystal
self

Intimacy

sometimes I get it reading Rilke

the small glimmer of sunlight
from the window
which rests
between your neck & the pillow

insight about how our fault-ridden bodies
are designed to shed, regrow & forget

how we both sleep better after sex
but we're both too tired to initiate

you can tell when a reference is second-hand
like when halfway through a movie
you realise you've rented it before

the haircut changes the shape of your face
the humidity the quality of your skin

now soft to touch
but strong, firm, young
perfect

some letters he wrote just to say
sorry for not writing sooner
there was this war I got held up in

No Country for Old Men

at the reading I was thinking
how can I afford to keep drinking
like a poet?   because that's what poets do
   think   I mean   & thinking these priceless thoughts
that are priceless in the way a toddler glues coloured macaroni
to a piece of paper & the kindergarten teacher says

      your budding aesthetic sensibilities
      have an intrinsic value that is
      worth more than money

I'm at a loss
        see   my parents love it
—the macaroni (*so* colourful)—they love it less
when I come home at 2am on a Wednesday
29 years old whispering myself up the stairs
to make very bourgeois sandwiches in the light of their refrigerator
            that's not what I wanted this poem to be about
but like sand in a pair of Docs worn to the beach
it manages to find a way in & ruin your life   Capitalism
   like a very persistent mosquito
buzzing around your head   biting you until you acquiesce
& start monetising all your hobbies   (all this for a prize?)
   it started   (all great schemes do)   at the bar
where I was standing with Banjo James
& maybe it was because we were
in the middle of making jokes about Les Murray
but suddenly all the old men looked just like cows heading
out to pasture   being poked & prodded by their minders
Banjo   stood looking like he always does
bearded & blue collar-ish possessing all the charm
& menace of Javier Bardem in that movie by the Coen Brothers
said   *don't worry mate   our turn will come*
—anyway I let Banj buy the beers

see   being a young poet & having no money is sort of a blessing
but in the more literal Judeo–Christian sense
where no one believes anything you do has value
until you've been dead for at least a hundred years

I trick myself into thinking I am usually reasonably productive
when I am hungover but this morning I am positively dying
& all my poems seem really pointless so I end each one with
then I found $50

I don't know   is it possible to be both pretentious
& sincere?   saturnine & prosperous?

I wanted this poem to be more hopeful, Banj
then I found $50

A Roman Holiday

a plot with cracks so big you can put your hand through them
big enough to scare Audrey Hepburn into thinking you aren't acting
tourists hang around buying old Roman coins you can't buy anything with
while we reach the end of a very long line for a frankly soggy pizza
like red sauce staining my white linen shirt I know you'll never leave me
I don't have to throw you over my shoulder into the Fontana di Trevi
though your eyes turn exactly that colour (turquoise & dazzling)
when you get that close to money / that far away from home
losing track of time & when I think I'm taking us somewhere unique
we end up back at the same café by the convertible church where I drink
the best coffee I've ever had altering my definition now I've had the real thing
I start re-enacting the scenes you like best until you physically restrain me
from hiring a vespa & I'm only convinced when you remind me I'm no good
cursing in Italian—who needs conversation when you've got car horns?
putting our lives in the hands of other road users & Romantics
the footpath is drenched in so much ancient light it almost makes you sick
with nostalgia—the way I keep spilling champagne on your trousers
            you figure something must be up
            no one goes to this much effort for a bad joke

Buried Verse

beneath our radiant   second verse
   there's more grist for those who
         try to bridge   the 'great' political
                 divide
yet
   the ham-fisted   pop-philosophy
tailored to the   silent majority
         slips   into the cracks
& fissures of   this abyss   roughly
   the size of   the desk
      on Q&A   seeping into the drinking water
     like fluoride   to keep our teeth white
                sharp
                 & pearly white
     I grip firmly
   to this $7 bottle of wine
that I bought instead of buying groceries
   yelling at the television   on a Monday night
wondering   how many Egyptians died
         building the pyramids
     from the top down
                    where ScoMo sits
             most uncomfortably
     atop that paragon   arrogantly
declaiming us the most successful
   multicultural nation in the world
as if it were an olympic sport
             (tho we all know we'd have
              a better chance of winning
              if it were the comm games)

looking confused & daggy
 as any politician would getting
actual sand in his boots—it's like
    Napoleon's soldiers   shelling off the nose of the sphinx
breathing a collective sigh of relief when
on the back of a dirty postcard a digger writes
 postcolonial   & doesn't get called up   on it

        the sick logic of this being
that   while skin abounds in our   sunburnt country being so
    sensitive & white   means getting stuck on whether to
            stock up or not: choosing vitamin D over aloe vera

girt by increased borders of self-preservation
   retreating indoors to complain safely about migration
people wait it out   in suburbs   sparse   & plain

        like a buried verse in an anthem
only ever mumbled   by overpaid athletes
       words   get lost in their delivery

   though it's clear   if Andrew Bolt keeps
talking   & people keep letting him   I don't think
            we'll ever be able to   reverse the effects   of such
                        awful coral bleaching

SS Ute as a Mood Ring

(After Aidan Coleman's 'Secondary')

the lights do not change from amber to green
although in Australia this afternoon
this SS ute descries that exact colour
the colour of road rage: an impatient radioactive throb
the driver's foot pumping up & down on the throttle
like a bystander's neck or the neck
of a semitransparent green bottle
as amber liquid gets poured from it
& is sloshed   all over the street
perhaps they're only driving benignly home
after a couple of bevies but this incessant revving
suggests or rather indicates that they're trying to drag me
at the intersection   it turns my mood ring
a colour as palatable as drink driving
the kind of combination that should be kept separate
or at least confined to the 80s
when almost anything was tolerated
as long as you could walk in a straight line

Whale Song (Minutt for Minutt)

to think that I could have been your cure for loneliness, but am not—like the channel on Norwegian television streaming continuous footage from cameras mounted to a cruise ship—folk songs, table service & old people leaning over the hull to watch whales surfacing in the bay—I could have been those whales for you—your foray into relative obscurity, the pastel in your pastel grey—the whales popping up to say

when you sing don't let your song be sad

The Rock Stars are Dying

Paul Simon says

a National guitar is an apt simile
but if you want my reflections
on rock and roll

   the rock stars are dying
soloing their way up the fretboard
towards the afterlife

    there's stars on 45
  & ash in Paisley Park
admittedly I've not ziggied
any stardust
in a while
                 but if Keith
        who once snorted his
      own father (!)
          says he is clean, man
       then what the hell
         so am I

Mick says
'this a poem I'd like to read for Brian:

we decay / like corpses in a charnel'

    older than bong water
or that crusty Led Zeppelin poster
in the shed above the drum kit
  covered in dust

you only had to be able to keep a beat
   & 30 pints of lager in your gullet
to be a drummer in the 70s
       racing to an early death

         like hate-reading
On The Road because we owe it to America
to stick our fingers down its chauvinistic guts
and marvel at the vomit of words

rock remains as age appropriate
as dating a 13 year old groupie
(Jimmy Page)
         —in that sense
   rock and roll royalty
is more Prince Andrew than Prince

should this serve as a symbol?
   a sign o the times?
should we not be toppling statues
out the front of concert venues too?

      you want it darker?
asks an album cover
      masquerading as an epitaph

before punk
before emo
there was The Rolling Stones
shouting 'paint it black!'
~ from a time when
    perhaps they meant their faces ~
     before the Stones there was
     the blues
          black music

and before that only
black musicians tuning up
    waiting to invent music

you can't ignore the erasure
 the damage
    or the war
but at the very least I guess
you can change the name
like Lady Antebellum
  to Lady A
        following a lawsuit

all the way to Graceland

        if male musicians treated women
    half as well as they treated their guitars
        rock wouldn't be so synonymous
            with misogyny

(this poem, not much of a requiem mass I'll admit
  but what do you expect for a genre typified
    by a bunch of teenagers dutching out a rec room?)

        rock and roll
        I gave you
        all the best years
        of my life

don't fear the reaper
  death comes quietly
you'll hardly hear it over the tinnitus

rock music didn't teach us
 anything
        really

Q: what's the difference between a zombie
        and a deadhead?
A: the money for a concert ticket

popular opinion suggests
rock and roll died years ago
but the music lives on
in dorm rooms
reclining on a beanbag
coughing, holding a spliff up
like a torch above an unwashed head
as pentatonic riff
follows pentatonic riff

I will always admire the way
Leonard Cohen
took a knee to bow
before the talent
of one of the musicians he employed
as they played a solo
        all class

whereas Ryan Adams fed on the souls
and careers of younger female artists
both pyrrhic and vampiric

        prickish

& that's how
the whole thing ended
sleeping upside down
like that roadie in Wayne's World

long live rock and roll

                    or maybe
        let it live and let die

rock and roll is dead

performing
the postmortem
post Malone

Late Night Thoughts

you're on a train looking out the window at all the things you said
but didn't really mean

past all the jokes you laughed at without really understanding them

all the jokes you told that weren't so much jokes
as microaggressions of truth

> a long tunnel approaches
>   you pass through it

travelling at great speed beneath the immense weight of all the things
you said in an argument that came out of your mouth before you
really knew what you were saying

> the train shows no sign of stopping

past all the times you said you'd read an article when you'd only read
the headline

by all the messages you saw but didn't answer

& the loyalty schemes you signed up to only to harbour years of
frustration at all the spam

poems fly past that were better in the dream than they were in the first
draft

chances you had to connect with other humans but chose the internet
instead

posts you retweeted drunk

rounds of drinks bought for you that you never got to pay back

amber lights you drove through knowing they were red

>   looking around for one of those emergency brakes to pull
>   & you realise there's no one else in the carriage:
>
>   only you
>
>   the lack of other voices is shocking

like every time you rapped the n word

>   in the silence   your heart skips a beat at the thought

no   you wouldn't ever again

>   the sound of the wheels against the rails
>   grinds out a rhythm   a pulse

every Penguin Classic you lied about finishing

every time you nodded confidently in the seminar about Bruno Latour

every Bergman film you lied about enjoying

the 'intermediate' French on your résumé

>   & then suddenly

you're sitting on a train looking out of the window

why a train?

Minor Seconds

listening to my own listless heart beating & you
beside me I discover we are minor seconds apart
tragic-chromatic   but if subtle harmony does exist
it's a three-year-old playing fists   palms & elbows
we manage to stay out of each other's way mostly
save for collateral clashes/catastrophes: collisions
& rhythms? look at this ventricular wall I put up
meaning: I stay regularly irregular   (always on time)
not jazz or syncopation   but syncope   synecdoche:
tickling the ivories 'you are the music until the music
stops' & with the train approaching the boom gates'
chiasmus suggests crossed purposes   my piano
teacher's arm reaching across me   she played the
C# and I the C   our fingers almost touching when
she said   'that's it there, you'll never forget it now'

Above Us the Great Grave Sky

(After Arthur Streeton)

1.

above us   the great grave sky

above us   the abstract ominous
hope inflected past
perfect continuous

above us   the singular metaphor
ascends prophetic
brushed with meaning

above us   the keen clear song
you bring to love
the irresolute present

nameless
you will be given a name

as the moment slips past
tenseless

2.

        restless
goosebumps
as the temperature drops
        starts dropping
my stomach
            the pits
        excited fizz
taken to the surface
a body admired
the sun goes down
on the horizon
without an anorak
 a scarf or
anything smart to say
nothing yet
to tie our strange
bodies in twain
an expectation of
instead I shift
uncomfortably
        helpless
insatiably distracted

love—that chill
on your skin
your bare shoulders
grabs you by
takes you
takes all of your
attention

3.

tension
when you blink
I take the moment
of reprieve
to remind myself
this isn't a date

stop blinking

stop

4.

spot any other
canvas you might like to take
you can have it
but this one I agonise over
altering each nuanced
expression of their bodies
the scrub   the moon
    these lovers
you can have it
once they become
just brushstrokes
again

5.

(when I find it)

my first love's
gonna be my last

(I have never waned)

my first love's
gonna be my last

6.

pastoral
   twilight pastoral
pastoral
             idyll
twilight pastoral
Heidelberg

7.

urgently naked
        beneath five
maybe six   blankets
Canberra's coldest
night   as fog waits
on median strips
to pass the night
roads widely anti
-cipating this thousand
year city   among
vast scrub retained
over years of pur-
posed pastoralisation
frost on the gum tree
a hangover
inherited from
our neighbours
as the sun hit the
aluminium rims
of our tins at
twilight   we saw
an amber flare
with amorous eyes
we took with us
to bed   we don't need
need Keats or Byron
            as below
        the moon
          below the
    clouds
        below these
blankets
            it's you

8.

from the spot where we last
lay dreaming together—yourself
and I—the soft grass beneath
us gleaming

above us   the great grave sky

Beginning & Ending with a Line from Hera Lindsay Bird

love comes back
    harder
falling in love with you
for the second time
is trying to sail back to the harbour
against a headwind
that I hardly felt as a tailwind
sailing out
        so confident
though I've never been on a boat
it's perfect saying things like
'catch my drift?'
    & you do
how did I get here?
       & now
how do I get back?
how careless of me
to have arrived at this party
so overexcited
   but so emotionally
  underprepared
(is anyone ever just
   'whelmed'?)
promising myself
these spirits (clearly)
too much for just
one person alone
although I really
go in for that feeling
 where I weigh

                nothing
            at the top
of the trampoline's vault
        when the valium
counterbalances the molly
            when left
        to my own devices
                            I sense
my back's against the wall
            though I know
I've never looked cool
standing alone at a party
I stumble outside
to feel the same wind
from earlier in the poem
hit me suddenly
        & when that rush subsides
lying down
                the trampoline
        stops bouncing
                    the boat stops pitching
love returns

Riffs

love comes back
like your father
twenty years later with the packet of
cigarettes he went out for
—Hera Lindsay Bird, *Love Comes Back*

love blows back
into an air hostesses' face
like a man on a plane being told
he's not allowed to vape
or a dolphin

love grows back
like a skinks tail
or the skin on an index finger which tried
interrupting a stick blender's
monologue

love goes flat
like a phone during a music festival
just as the cap kicks in
& you get separated from your friends

love backs up
like a hard drive
or a hilux over a
razor scooter in a driveway

love gives back
like a wealthy CEO
avoiding tax

love with no take backs
like an email with a spelling mistake
like an email with only spelling mistakes
like an email with no text at all

love fights back
like a duck

love bites back
telling you hickeys are boring
& that your foreplay has become
unimaginative

love changes tack
like discovering you know nothing
about yachts & cannot complete
the metaphor

love calls back
but your phone has been stolen
by a tuk-tuk driver
& they answer
very confused

love backs away
but the audience knows
the killer is really
behind the door
waiting

love punches back
like a hockey player
in lieu of playing hockey

love turns its back
on a promising career
in the name of pursuing true love

love comes back
it all comes back
to love

Bar Bazzanti (Italian Opera)

overture

my dream a drink with the cyclone
where we are discussing weather patterns
paintings & the sky
the way the waves push
against the cliffs
beneath the Castello
where the old part of Gaeta
pokes out into the Tyrrhenian
like a trochaic foot
severed at the ankle broken
off of a statue toppled
in a storm or in a revolution
& this is all that remains

aria da capo

I don't do things in halves
between the seen & the remembered
in the borrowed light
from a poem by Cavafy
these same tables & chairs
belonging to a taverna long closed
but vivid now
I order a bottle of blanco
not doing things in halves

I am open to the night
its live changes
at ease in the residual heat

of its surface
shifting between the
different scenes
evening setting
with great drinking
comes great possibility
I give in to those
half-real moments
bright energy
incandescence
into it I go
as the night opens up

I don't do things in halves
drinking as one
who is unafraid of pleasure
drinks   —as one who
is remembering the feeling
recovers that lost part
of themselves half
remembered
drinks

chorus

by the sea by the sea
how happy we will be
at the bar bazzanti

ensemble

families ease past without
a second glance
fishermen

send out one line apiece
for something to do
with their hands
two men smoking cigars
behind us
their raspy voices
as coarse as their inhalations
young men leaning on
their vespas
whistling at a group of girls
across the street
sitting on a park bench texting
giggling

typically late season
where the gelato store is open
but not busy
the girl behind the counter
watches television on her phone
the sound spills into the square

looping around
the public bus
from the old part of town
threading the needle
of history
taking itself back
every half an hour
puffing past us
the driver switches
on the headlights

old vinyl seats
the light from the

curved streetlamp
sticking to them
the way age sticks
to us all

chorus

by the sea by the sea
how happy we will be
at the bar bazzanti

duo

PAINTER kicks the chair out from under the table without acknowledging the arrival of his guest

POET: so you worked today?

PAINTER: the light wasn't right

WAITER arrives carrying a bottle of white wine and a glass placing both in front of the POET

POET: does that happen often?

PAINTER pouring wine into both their glasses

PAINTER: more often than you'd think

(silence)

POET picks up glass and holds it around head height

POET: what should we toast to?

PAINTER: to this   to being here
        & to no more questions
        let the silence do its work

Nice Things, Artfully Arranged

this poem I read starts

       that reminds me

as if all poems didn't start with that premise
anyway
       anyway

       that reminds me
     of a girlfriend I had once
who   had this terrifyingly beautiful
   almost translucent skin

       & who through no one's fault
    would bruise *like a peach*

always   wearing black tights to cover her shins
& thighs   as if this clumsiness   accidentally knocking
into things   was a   *statement of intent*

   I was reading this article about flower arrangement
(I know)   & the symbolism inherent

   like—they're never *just* lilies   but rather

       vectors of condolence

when my Maminka died
    my uncle's friend   thoughtfully
   sent a bowl of fruit to the wake   which made

me laugh because I thought

what could be worse
than crying tears into a fucking
kiwifruit?

if you'd never seen a kiwifruit
you'd think
that's a pretty shitty kinder surprise

do these trifles exist if I never tell you?
does this kit kat
that I'm eating
on the way home
if I hide the wrapper
in my pocket?

remember me telling you
about Heiko   the enthusiastic manager
we had   in Germany
pushing us onto the stage in Greifswald?
he said:

don't forget to tell them how big you are back home!

will this translate?
does it leave a mark?

bruises
I feel   are like accidental transfers
temporary tattoos

birthmarks
like unwanted
& permanent ones

drawing our eyes away
like this garnish does   from the
   inevitable selection of cold meats
      at the wake

           creating diversions
     the way butterflies do
  from the fact that they are
                  really
      just moths

     I wonder if there's a job
for someone with a PhD in English
    pairing vases with flowers
  to accentuate the symbolism?

shedding light on the less obvious

how do I go fitting all this in
one poem?

       too many flowers
       for this vase

anyway   *you* can tell I don't care
about the dishes being clean

it's just easier than making conversation
with awkward relatives
             scrubbing the dishes
    & wiping my hands on my good jeans

        leaving such a small trace

Notes

'The Coffee Coffee Drinks': The word Maminka means 'mother' in Slovak and is the name we called my late grandmother Anna T Vnuk (nee Flaherty) who married my very Slovak grandfather František (Apinko) in 1956 despite his preference for Latin over English. I haven't seen the necklace but it must have been good.

'Fucking Adelaide': 'Glass of water?' references a note passed by Dennis Denuto in 'The Castle' (1997). Ezra Pound (that old fascist) did once say that 'Poetry requires the energy of a lifetime', but I don't know where. Skyshow was a fireworks display synchronised to music that ran in the Adelaide parklands from 1985—2006. As public transport was free that night some teenagers used to smuggle goon bags under their jumpers and ride busses into the city.

'Scattole Personali': The original title for this poem was September. This current title references a series of works by American artist Robert Rauschenberg, first displayed in Rome in 1952. *Scattole personali* (or 'personal boxes') were laid on the floor of a Roman exhibition space containing different knick-knacks he had picked up from the flea markets. Attendees were invited to take whatever caught their eye home with them. This poem wouldn't have been possible without Tim Wright's 'November' from *The Night's Live Changes* (Rabbit, 2014) or Melody Paloma's 'October' from *In Some Ways Dingo* (Rabbit, 2017).

'Above Us the Great Grave Sky': This ekphrastic poem takes its name from the painting by Arthur Streeton, who took the title of his painting from 'Doubtful Dreams', a poem by Adam Lindsay Gordon. The final stanza of my poem is an excerpt, appearing as it did the first time I saw the painting at the National Gallery of Australia in Canberra. 'My first love's gonna be my last' is a lyric from the song 'Alaska' by Banjo Jackson from the album *Banjo Jackson* (2015).

'Bar Bazzanti': This poem takes the form of an opera, set in the bar where Cy Twombly drank in Gaeta. There are two signed Twombly exhibition posters above the door. On one of them he has scrawled 'by the sea by the sea / how happy we will be / at the bar bazzanti'. The tavern from Cavafy's 'I Went' is referenced in this poem, but really all of his poems take place in nondescript, dimly lit taverns, so use your imagination.

Acknowledgements

I acknowledge the Kaurna people as the traditional owners of the land where many of these poems were written. I would also like to acknowledge the Wurundjeri Woi Wurrung people of the Kulin Nation as the traditional owners of the land where this manuscript was completed. Sovereignty was never ceded. Australia always was, always will be aboriginal land and I pay my respects to elders past, present and emerging.

A number of these poems in different iterations were published in various journals and anthologies, including *Apeiron Review*, *Australian Book Review*, *Australian Poetry Anthology*, *Axon*, *Cordite Poetry Review*, *Demos Journal*, *Marrickville Pause*, *Meniscus*, *Overland*, *Rabbit*, *Saltbush Review*, *Social Alternatives*, *Spineless Wonders*, *StylusLit* and *Best of Australian Poems 2021*. My thanks to all the editors and publishers for their tireless work to keep Australian poetry alive.

'Sonnet (Now Now)' and 'Hallelujah Junction' appear in the chapbook *Now Now* published by Garron Press in their Southern Poets Series, 2018. My thanks to Gary and Sharon. 'Fucking Adelaide', 'A Roman Holiday', and 'Minor Seconds' appear in the chapbook *Minor Seconds* published by Little Windows Press in 2018. My thanks to Alison and Jill.

Many of these poems were debuted at the No Wave reading series at The Wheatsheaf Hotel in Thebarton. My sincere thanks to Olivia, Gemma and Banjo for helping out, to all those poets who have read at No Wave, and to everyone who regularly attends for making the community of poets in Adelaide vital and inspiring.

I am very grateful to Ken Bolton for his honest, and sometimes too honest, appraisal of this manuscript in various stages. That same gratitude extends to Jill Jones for being an all-time punk genius. Without Jill's encouragement there would be no book. And finally, thanks to Shane Strange and the team at Recent Work Press for believing in these poems and for seeing them through.

This book is dedicated to the Vadasz Family. Sorry for all the swear words.

About the Author

Dominic Symes lives and writes in Naarm (Melbourne). He curates NO WAVE, a monthly poetry reading series, on Kaurna Country (Adelaide) where he grew up. Most recently he was selected for Cordite/AP's 'Tell me like you mean it 4' anthology and the 'Best of Australian Poems 2021' anthology. 'I saw the best memes of my generation' is his first collection of poetry.

www.ingramcontent.com/pod-product-compliance
Ingram Content Group Australia Pty Ltd
76 Discovery Rd, Dandenong South VIC 3175, AU
AUHW020639050325
407891AU00002B/13

9 780645 356366